PHIT for LIFE

Find Purpose While You Lose Weight Naturally & Spiritually

Tiffany James

Written Words Publishing LLC
14189 E Dickinson Drive, Unit F
Aurora, CO 80014
www.writtenwordspublishing.com

PHIT for LIFE © 2020 by Tiffany James.

All rights reserved. No part of this publication may be reproduced, stored in a retrieval system, or transmitted in any form by any means, electronic, mechanical, photocopying, recording, or otherwise, without the prior permission of the author.

Published by Written Words Publishing LLC 6/4/2020

ISBN: 978-1-7332357-2-3 (paperback)
ISBN: 978-1-7332357-3-0 (eBook)

Library of Congress Control Number: 2020909953

Cover designed by Written Words Publishing LLC

Manufactured and printed in the United States of America

All Scripture quotations, unless otherwise indicated, are taken from the King James Version of the Bible, public domain. Scripture quotations noted as NKJV are taken from the New King James Version. Copyright © 1979, 1980, 1982 by Thomas Nelson, Inc. Used by permission. All rights reserved. Scripture quotations noted as NLT are taken from the Holy Bible, New Living Translation, Copyright © 1996, 2004, 2007. Used by permission of Tyndale House Publishers, Inc., Carol Stream, Illinois 60188. All rights reserved. Scripture quotations noted as AMP are taken from the Amplified® Bible (AMP), Copyright © 2015 by The Lockman Foundation. Used by permission of The Lockman Foundation. All rights reserved worldwide. Scripture quotations noted as NIV are taken from the Holy Bible, New International Version® NIV®. Copyright © 1973, 1978, 1984, 2011 by the International Bible Society. Used by permission of Zondervan Publishing House. All rights reserved worldwide. Scripture quotations marked CEV are from the Contemporary English Version Copyright © 1991, 1992, 1995 by American Bible Society. Used by Permission. Scripture quotations noted as MSG are taken from *The Message*. Copyright © 1993, 1994, 1995, 1996, 2000, 2001, 2002. Used by permission of NavPress Publishing Group. Scripture quotations marked CSB have been taken from the Christian Standard Bible®, Copyright © 2017 by Holman Bible Publishers. Used by permission. Christian Standard Bible® and CSB® are federally registered trademarks of Holman Bible Publishers.

TABLE OF CONTENTS

Introduction 1

Heavyweights 6

Becoming PHIT 12

Weights in the Spirit and the Natural 22

The Right Attitude and Heart 25

His Grace Will Help You Overcome 29

PHIT for LIFE Health Tips 34

PHIT for LIFE Healthy Meals 36

PHIT for LIFE Shrimp Egg Rolls Recipe 37

PHIT for LIFE Shrimp and Spinach Salad Recipe 38

PHIT for LIFE Turkey Bacon Vegetable Quiche Recipe 39

PHIT for LIFE Homemade Breakfast Pizza 40

PHIT for LIFE Homemade Vegetable Meat Pizza 41

PHIT for LIFE Pineapple and Kale Juice 42

PHIT for LIFE Strawberry Ginger Lemonade Juice 43

PHIT for LIFE Apple Cucumber with Celery Juice 44

PHIT for LIFE Banana Smoothie 45

PHIT for LIFE Blueberry Spinach Smoothie 46

PHIT for LIFE Kiwi Strawberry Smoothie 47

Exercise Tips..48

PHIT for LIFE Exercise Plans 49

About the Author...52

INTRODUCTION

Today, in our society many people are struggling with various challenges. Low self-esteem, financial problems, anger issues, unforgiveness, addictions, depression, and weight problems. Some of these negative challenges seem to connect and bring people down to their lowest of lows. I do believe I have unlocked a concealed truth that will encourage you today and will help you become PHIT for LIFE.

The acronym PHIT stands for <u>Physical Health Inspirational Training</u>. If we can become more PHIT, we will be able to overcome many of the challenges we face in life, especially when it comes to our weight and overall health. Unfortunately, at times, because of some of the negative things we go through and the negative pressures we feel from others, it's hard to be successful and measure up to what society or people say you are supposed to be like.

Many years ago, while exercising and working out, I didn't realize I discovered a major key to the many struggles people tend to deal with when they are trying to lose weight. I have and still do have a great personal trainer; I will talk more about him in the book later. Throughout the years, I have written many notes about what I learned and experienced in my own life and my journey while losing weight. I am so excited and happy to share them with you as you read my book.

I must warn you that this is not your ordinary weight loss book. This is not just your average read. This book is filled with life-changing secrets that will transform you internally, externally and ultimately eternally. Many weight loss books promise certain results, not realizing every person's make-up, DNA and framework is different and unique. Because every person is different in their own special way, every person needs their own unique weight loss plan designed just for them.

Many commercials, ads, and books give people a false illusion about the course of action a person may need to take to reach their weight loss goals. People often get caught up looking at before and after pictures of someone who has lost weight. But, they don't pause and take inventory of details which happened in between the before and after. My objective is not only to get you excited about how you will look and feel after you lose weight (that is one of the goals for sure), but the center of my attention will also focus on the in between process. There is so much to learn about yourself during the in between process. When you learn to endure and not just go through a fad for instamatic success, you develop strong roots.

I have learned from my own experiences that when you have strong roots you can build a strong foundation. People with a strong foundation usually have patience. It's okay to be patient because while you are in a waiting season of your life, you can develop your character, mature and grow from your mistakes.

I believe for certain, if we live long enough, sometimes we will encounter stumbling blocks, hurdles and various issues that all together may cause us to stop pursuing our overall goal. Roadblocks and setbacks are not the end; they are just a stepping stone to one of your many greatest victories. You may say to yourself, "Well how do you know that? What makes you an expert concerning this?" Well, I am a living-breathing example of what happens when you continue to trust the greatest expert. We can't overcome by ourselves. We need help while we are pursuing our goals.

"I press on to reach the end of the race and receive the heavenly prize for which God, through Christ Jesus, is calling us" (Philippians 3:14 NLT).

My focus is to talk about weight loss, but during the process of losing weight, there is so much to discover about you and the makeup of who you really are. Many times, people go through life never really understanding their purpose in life. They don't have a complete understanding that God does not make accidents and there is an assignment for them to fulfill. Greatness is in all of us and God sometimes will use peculiar and even uncomfortable situations to show how great He really is in your life. The awesome thing about the opposition we experience in our lives and everyday situations is we have been given an opportunity for purpose to be manifested. Opposition is an opportunity for you to be blessed. It is a time for you to discover you and it is a time for your purpose to be revealed.

Usually, the process we go through to get to our destiny is uncomfortable and does not always feel good. Anytime a person experiences something out of their norm (whatever your normal maybe), it does not feel good emotionally or physically. Just because things are not going the way you think they should go, that does not mean God's perfect plan for your life isn't being fulfilled.

When a baby is learning to walk, they tend to fall down. The key is they get back up and try again even though they may hurt themselves. Why do they get back up? Because even babies know when it is time to go to the next level. God has supernaturally created us all and down deep inside of us *"God has apportioned to each a degree of faith [and a purpose designed for service]"* (Romans 12:3 AMP). Babies even know there is more to life than the crawl phase and that's where the measure of faith kicks into gear. The same principle of faith mixed with God's love and grace can be applied to our weight loss process. If you keep pushing, if you keep pressing and keep trying, you will eventually reach your goal.

Everyone's process while losing weight and maintaining their weight loss is different. I want to encourage you, as you read this book, to think of yourself as a champion. Champions train their thoughts; they rely on the word of God to give them strength. *"Keep this Book of the Law always on your lips; meditate on it day and night, so that you may be careful to do everything written in it. Then you will be prosperous and successful"* (Joshua 1:8 NIV). Champions understand and are familiar with their weaknesses, but they also know how to worship God and submit to His spirit so they can be strengthened and learn. What had you down once before cannot keep you down.

No one is perfect; we tend to mess up and make mistakes occasionally as we journey through life. If you ever speak with a true champion about how they became successful, most of them will share how they learned and became better from their failures. The more I pray and read God's word, the more I understand how awesome, powerful and sovereign the Lord, Jesus Christ is. Our God is a champion and you came from a champion. The dictionary defines champion as a person who has defeated or surpassed all rivals in competition. So, even when your situation looks gloomy and you feel like nothing good can ever come out of what you are going through, you must remember that every season is your season and your time to shine. There is always grace for us to win and get back up again. You might not understand everything now, but your heavenly father knows *"the thoughts that I think toward you, saith the Lord, thoughts of peace, and not of evil, to give you an expected end"* (Jeremiah 29:11 KJV).

Setting outrageous goals with a microwave thinking mentality often causes people to fall short of their desired weight loss goals. We have to remember overnight success is not always beneficial. We may have obtained or reached our weight loss goal, but do we have the mindset and positive lifestyle to maintain the weight loss goal we reached?

I believe, if we stay connected to the one true living God and walk in His grace daily, all things are possible for the one who believes and trusts in Jesus. (Mark 9:23 AMP)

HEAVYWEIGHTS

When most people think about losing weight, they usually become very discouraged about the process. Others start, but some become frustrated and quit. Why? Because they don't see the immediate results they want. (It's kind of like when I am in an uncomfortable situation and God is taking too long concerning my situation, I will just do things my way).

Some people hang in there for a while and soon get to the point of "My life is too busy right now and I don't have enough discipline to keep this up." Maintaining a healthy weight for your body (notice I said, for you) and healthy lifestyle is very significant to your overall well-being. Being well in your body is essential to fulfilling your purpose and destiny.

Many people want to lose weight in their physical body, so they can look good. What a lot of people don't realize is that there are many other benefits that come from losing weight and maintaining a healthy life. Some of those benefits include self-confidence, discipline, healthy doctor reports, freedom, reduced stress, more money, and a better wardrobe. The process and the journey to losing weight can show you who you really are and jump-start you into your purpose for life.

It is so easy to pick up weight naturally. Everywhere we go from billboard signs, magazines, cell phones, and televisions, we are constantly seeing advertisements about food. Comfort foods such as sugary snacks have become a crutch for many of us when we are trying to get through the day; or, if we had a terrible day, a sugary snack will help calm our nerves at the end of the day. Our country has prided itself on having larger portions and excessive fatty foods. Regular exercising usually is not on the mind of most people because they wake up early to go to work and after working long hours, they are usually exhausted. Going to the gym after work or exercising at home is not on their agenda. Many families use their leisure time to rest and are distracted by social media or video games. We are currently living in a world that has numerous ways to get our attention off the real reason and purpose of why we are here. Experiencing an overload from all the distractions in our society not only can have us worn down and tired, but it can have us spiritually depleted.

So, not only do we pick up weight naturally (just from the stresses of life), we also pick up weight spiritually. Regardless of how you picked up weight, it can leave you heavy and make you feel burdened down. Sometimes, we pick up so many weights, we don't know where or how we became so entangled in a bunch of mess.

What you eat affects your natural body weight. What you take into your spirit man through your eyes, ears, and mouth weighs on your spirit man. What you do physically you have to do spiritually. Exercising your physical body is a necessity, but you also need to exercise in the spirit.

Some years back, I was discouraged about my workout routine. I wasn't losing weight like I wanted to. Sometimes, when we hit a stumbling block, we want an easy quick fix. All of my other methods of losing weight were not working. So, I decided to sincerely pray and have a conversation with the Lord about my weight problems.

I prayed, "Lord, help me lose weight."
He said, "I want you to lose weight."
I said, "Okay, I'm ready!"

Then the Lord ministered to me and said, "But I'm not just talking about physical weight. I want you to lay aside every weight that so easily besets you. Weights of stress, feeling overwhelmed, fear, anxiety, not feeling good enough, not measuring up, frustration from your jobs, frustration from your children; lay aside those weights."

So, I said, "Okay. How do I lay aside those weights?"

And when I asked that question, the Lord ministered to me, "You are going to have to learn to exercise in the spirit and the natural. Denying your flesh in the natural and the spirit sometimes doesn't feel good. Sometimes it can even hurt, but the end result is Beautiful. When you feel like you can't go anymore and you are weak in your natural man, this scripture will help."

"My body and mind may fail, but you are my strength and my choice forever" (Psalm 73:26 CEV). God is the part of you that makes you whole; if you rely on His strength, especially when you are weak, you can never go wrong.

One of the keys to losing weight in the natural and the spirit is maintaining the right mindset and heart. God created man in His own image (His likeness) and He created you and me to reveal His heart to us. Knowing God's love and His heart will reveal your heart. Fellowship and relationship with God will remove your old heart and give you a new heart. Your new heart has to exercise and beat after God's heart or you will revert back to your old ways and habits. How do you keep your new heart? You guessed it, exercise! Exercise your mind by reading and meditating on the scriptures. What do the scriptures say about exercising? *"For physical training is of some value, but godliness (spiritual training) is of value in everything and in every way, since it holds promise for the present life and for the life to come"* (I Timothy 4:8 AMP).

Exercise is doing an activity of some kind, and giving a physical effort to complete a purpose relevant to your health and fitness. Usually, when we think about exercise, we think of some vigorous workout we have to continuously do to become fit. But that is not always the case. We have to have a balance in everything we do, or we will get burned out and eventually quit altogether.

Sometimes, the physical exercise we do is just maintenance for our bodies and that is okay. We can't always get caught up on unrealistic goals. Depending on how much weight you need to lose, you have to go at a pace that is right for you. So, if you don't see the results you want right then, you still have to learn how to encourage yourself. You have to say things to yourself like, "I didn't lose weight from that workout, but it did keep the extra pounds off." It's just like our walk with our Lord and Savior, Jesus Christ. If I want to touch God in a deep way, I may have to spend more time with Him and not just go to church on Sunday morning and expect the message to keep me in right standing for the rest of the week. This is a generation of people that want what they want right now (including myself). So, a quick easy fix for some people is to binge exercise and get it in all at one time instead of working out and exercising daily. Exercising has to be a part of your daily routine; it has to be an essential part of your lifestyle. You have to ask God for a desire and passion to become PHIT not just in your natural body, but in every area of life.

When your heart is strong and perfect towards the Lord, you are on the right track. Having a right heart towards the

Lord and the right attitude during the process of losing weight, adds more grace to your weight loss process. Now, you are ready to lose weight naturally and physically. There is grace for you if you mess up. It's okay if you do. Mishaps, setbacks, hang-ups, and failures are not the end. Remember, they are steppingstones to help you walk into your destiny and future.

You may ask the question, "So, how can I get my heart strong and perfect towards the Lord?" When God first made, designed and carefully put you together before your parents thought about having you, He made you perfect and designed you like himself. You were made whole with no blemishes. Nothing was missing, nothing was broken; you were carefully put together and made like no other. God made you with different talents and gifts for Him to be glorified, but those gifts are also inside you to be a blessing to you and others around you. One of the keys to having a strong and perfect heart towards the Lord is knowing who you are and who you belong to. If we don't know who we are, we are susceptible to fall for anybody and anything. It will cause us to add more heavyweights in our life.

Jesus was and is a gift to you. Now, the question is, what is your gift back to Him? Through my own experiences, I learned the best gift I can ever give back to Jesus is my heart, because He is the great creator and the one who originated me.

God blessed me with many talents and gifts, and over the past couple of years, I experienced many blessings because of them. The Lord put the gifts and talents inside of me when He first created me. And even though I only saw myself as an average person, the Lord knew when He made me, He was making something special. Some of the gifts and talents He put inside me, I discovered at a young age. Others came into manifestation when I became older and wiser.

The process of life will teach you who you are, and what you thought had you upside down can ignite a passion inside of you that will reveal one of your greatest talents yet to be seen by the world. Truly submitting my talents and my heart to the Lord has opened doors for me to be abundantly blessed spiritually and naturally.

BECOMING PHIT

I believe the Lord wants us to be healthy in every area of our life, which includes our emotions, relationships, body weight, finances, etc. Jesus died for us to live a complete, fulfilled, abundant life. Just because we go through a low place or a valley does not mean we will not come out victorious. God sometimes is just exercising our faith. We have a great external resource who is more than able to help us win. When I say win, what I mean is sometimes until you feel like you are a victim of your circumstances, you will never know the victor and who can bring you out.

Let me give you some insight about how PHIT for LIFE came into fruition. Until about 12 years ago, ever since I was a little girl growing up, all I could remember was several instances of struggling with my weight. I can recall cycles during my youth, teenage and college years of losing weight and then gaining it back.

I remember, back in elementary school, having a concert event after school. Our music instructor wanted us to look nice and wear certain colors. I had an outfit from a previous occasion, but it was too small. My mother bought me another outfit and even though I had new clothes on, I felt ashamed because I was a little overweight. I had a new outfit not because I got taller, but because my belly was too big for the other one. That incident made me feel like I was less than everyone else and I felt insignificant that night.

Sports throughout my youth, teenage and college years have always been a lifesaver for me when it came to losing weight. The downside for me though was when off season came, I didn't do the workouts because I didn't enjoy exercising on my own. During off-seasons from whatever sports I played, I usually ate anything and everything I wanted.

After gaining a good bit of weight after college and being back home for a while, I became serious about my weight loss, but my motives for losing weight were not right. After getting married and before I had my first child, I can say I was probably in the best shape of my life, but God also had to deal with me about the spirit of vanity. I worked out all the time (morning, noon and night); constantly weighing myself and a bit out of control with my workouts and very particular about what I ate. I didn't realize that I don't have to be perfect and I don't have to compare myself to anybody. The only voice that really matters at the end of the day is God's voice and what He says about me and my situation.

You have to understand that life is not all about you. If you are not careful, the spirit of pride can crawl into anything you do. God is the one who gives you grace to overcome and be successful in anything you do. You have to be careful that you always give God glory for the achievements and victories in your life.

A year or so after college, I got married and after a couple of years we had children. Having children caused me to gain weight again. After my first child, the weight came off in about 9 months, but I had to exercise frequently and eat healthy. The blessing was, I was in between jobs, so I had more time to exercise during mornings and afternoons. My second child was born while I was working a full-time job and I gained less weight because I had morning sickness (I say it was really an all-day sickness). It took about a year and a half to finally lose all the weight.

Both of those weight loss experiences ministered to me in many different ways. Having two children and losing weight the way God would want, caused me to reflect on other past ways I tried to lose weight. One thing I learned is our bodies are not stupid; they enjoy hanging on to fatty cells, especially as we tend to get older. Many people in their youth and early stages of life tend to rely on their own strength, which can only get them so far. Losing weight my way, after looking back over my life, always resulted in me gaining the weight back. But, when I finally got tired of the cycles, I decided to humble myself and say, "God, help me lose weight the way You designed for me to lose weight." Not only did He give me a plan for what I needed to do, He also gave me a desire to like working out. Remember earlier, when I told you that in high school I didn't do the summer workouts because I hated working out alone and by myself, it was boring to me? Now, because I asked God to be a part of my workout routine, he gave me a Godly passion for being healthy and physically fit. I enjoy working out and eating healthy foods a lot more than I used to. Don't get me wrong, I still eat sweets sometimes, but unhealthy choices do not control me.

The awesome thing is now when I work out, God speaks to me and encourages me. He strengthens me and helps me as I ask Him to. Jesus and I have intimate conversations about His love for me. He removes my doubts and fears while I'm running in my neighborhood or doing different exercises. When I dwell in the secret place of the most High God and abide under the shadow of the Almighty (Psalm 91:1 KJV), peace and understanding comes to help me through my day. And that's how PHIT for LIFE came into manifestation.

I have many stories about losing and gaining weight before the Lord gave me my personal PHIT for LIFE principles. I have also talked with others about their struggles while losing weight. Let's be honest, losing weight can be difficult; if it was easy, everyone would do it and be happy about their weight and appearance.

I know from my own experiences it stinks to lose weight and then gain it back. The ups and downs of trying so many different diets are exhausting, especially when you do not see the results you want. When I said earlier that I humbled myself and asked God to help me lose weight the way He wanted me to (in the spirit and the natural), I believe when I prayed that prayer selfish motives were removed from my heart. My goal no longer was just about losing weight and being seen as a person with a perfect body. My heart's cry to God became "I want to lose weight for Your glory. Help me learn how to fight this battle in the spirit and become healthy for the rest of my life."

"Those who think they can do it on their own end up obsessed with measuring their own moral muscle but never get around to exercising it in real life. Those who trust God's action in them find that God's Spirit is in them—living and breathing God! Obsession with self in these matters is a dead end; attention to God leads us out into the open, into a spacious, free life. Focusing on the self is the opposite of focusing on God. Anyone completely absorbed in self ignores God, ends up thinking more about self than God. That person ignores who God is and what He is doing. And God isn't pleased at being ignored" (Romans 8:5-8 MSG).

No matter what phase of your weight loss journey you are in, you have to speak life into yourself. Speak positive confessions despite what you may see naturally. Ask God daily to help see things spiritually. *"The tongue has the power of life and death, and those who love it will eat its fruit"* (Proverbs 18:21 NIV).

Don't let your present situation or your past determine your future. See yourself as a masterpiece and a great work of art. God already wrote your manuscript; He's just waiting on you to walk it out.

PHIT for LIFE is not just a fad you go through because it's what everybody is doing and popular for now. PHIT for LIFE has the word "life" in it because these are principles you can always come back to and use throughout the course of your life. Sometimes we just have to get back to the basics. Real joy, peace and love can be experienced while becoming PHIT. It is important to experience what's real and not get caught up with superficial stuff. You can lose weight and look really good but still be unhealthy, lack self-confidence, be confused mentally, and unhappy with life in general.

I have learned you can change your outer appearance in many ways even after you lose weight by changing your makeup, cutting your hair, changing your clothes and your shoes. But if you don't change internally and have an encounter with Jesus, more than likely you will entertain old habits and old ways that had you bound before.

If you are experiencing weight loss setbacks, then you need a PHIT for LIFE daily routine that is designed just for you. Everybody's plan is not the same. Why? Because everyone's physique is not the same. We all have our own special DNA; so, we have to consult with the great creator (the Lord, Jesus Christ).

Many questions have been asked when it comes to weight loss. Many theories and scientific facts have been put on the table and some of them worked for some people. But I believe I found the answer. So, how do you become successful in your weight loss journey? How do you find your purpose while going through uncomfortable and seemingly unfavorable circumstances and situations? Remember earlier, when I told you I have and still do have a great personal trainer? Well, His name is Jesus. The Holy Spirit is the one that helped me lose weight and maintain a healthy weight for my body frame.

Jesus (the Holy Spirit) is my personal trainer, coach, disciplinary, teacher, counselor, guide, and educator. One of the key components He taught me about weight loss is understanding the true definition of success. Often times, people relate their accomplishments to their identity, and their identity is not always defined by what they have accomplished or failed at. Social media has ruined people into thinking they have to be perfect. People have recreated themselves through different social media sites and, unfortunately, people think that is what I'm supposed to look like too. One of the most critical keys you need to know about becoming successful is you are the best you can ever be. You don't have to compare yourself to anybody. You are chosen and set apart for a reason. But it is okay to have flaws because there is a God who can help you with your imperfections. Your identity comes from God and what God alone says about you. His love for you is your identity. Ask yourself, do you define your achievements and failures based on popularity votes or are they based on what is eternal? If it is based on what is eternal, then you are already a winner. You know who you are, and you are who God says you are and not the negative things you have done in your past.

So, you might have to remind yourself from time to time, "I know I might not have accomplished everything I want to accomplish yet and that is okay." But there is one thing that I do know. The scripture teaches me in I John 4:19 (NIV), Jesus Christ first loved me. Because He first loved me, that means there is a promise on my life and I was made with a purpose.

I don't have to wait until I have accomplished something to declare who I am. God's design and plan for my life is already done and declared by His Spirit. His plan for my life just hasn't manifested in the natural yet.

Whatever you are just starting in your life, whether it's a new business, college, new job or losing weight, please remember God already finished it for you and made a way when He died on the cross over 2,000 years ago.

You have to make it a habit to remember that when you commit to your weight loss process naturally and spiritually, you already are somebody in Christ Jesus. If we embrace and ask God to help us enjoy climbing our ladder of success, we wouldn't get so frustrated at times when things don't always go our way, because we know that God ultimately has the best for us. *"I can do all this through him who gives me strength"* (Philippians 4:13 NIV). Renewing your mind with the word of God daily will cause your faith to rise and you can confidently say, "I know who I am."

Always identify who you are by His love for you. Understanding who you are in this way will help you when you have negative random images in your mind about yourself, especially when it seems like you are at the losing end when it comes to losing weight.

You see, the Lord's love is not like people love and He loves all of you (the inside and outside). He loves the big you, small you, medium you—it doesn't matter to Him and the great thing is God has grace for you and I while we are on this journey.

Do not get into the habit of identifying yourself by your appearance and how much you weigh, especially if you are struggling with your weight. If you do this, not only will you feel bad about your exterior features, but your self-esteem will be negatively impacted as well. Being spiritually healthy means you must identify yourself by what God says about you through His word; no matter how you feel, or what you see or have done. When you identify yourself this way and are open to God, His love for you will bring change to your heart. His nature is to love you and now He can minister to you personally on how to lose weight naturally and spiritually.

I personally don't believe when God first made us His intentions was for everyone to walk around this earth as skinny twig sticks and I also don't think His design for our body make up was for us to be overweight. Our image of what perfection is has been flawed by what we see on television and magazines.

The Bible says in the beginning God created the heavens and earth and He also made man. Adam was communicating with the animals and naming them. They could have anything they wanted except the tree of knowledge of good and evil. My understanding from that is they had some discipline, and successful people have some kind of discipline in their lives. I also think that Adam and Eve could have been vegetarians before they sinned. I'm not saying you need to be a vegetarian while you are trying to lose weight, but once God gives you a plan for your life, whether it is what you eat or how often you exercise, it is important to continue to be led by His direction in all that you do.

If you are having trouble, ask God to help you. He will give you grace and a desire to do things His way. Jesus died on the cross and rose from the dead (John 3:16 NIV) for us to have life and liberty. Some of us have been in too many of the same cycles only to get no where and we can't afford to reap any more negative consequences. When we ask God for His forgiveness and guidance, it helps us build a relationship with our Heavenly Father, which has always been God's intention.

God knows your body, your frames and make up, because He is the one who made you. So, He knows what's right for you including what you should be eating and not eating, and what exercise plan is good for you. He knows everything about you and how your body changes with time, and is concerned about you.

If your mind is healthy, you can get your body healthy. Heavy weights start in the mind and a lot of times end up manifesting in our natural body. There is a way for you and I to be free. A simply yes to His plans and His ways opens the door to the provision God has for us.

Your heart being open to God's ways is a setup for success. His supernatural strength on your natural limitations are always better. This way you are ready if your personal trainer (the Holy Spirit) speaks to you. Your personal trainer may say take a walk every other morning or He may say no eating after 8:00pm this week. He may even say drink water with every meal this week. Your workouts may be strenuous or light. Whatever it is you are told to do you can do it through Christ Jesus. Step by step, day by day—you can do it! You may have to ask God to help you not desire fatty foods as much and replace that thirst and desire with healthy foods, but it can be done.

WEIGHTS IN THE SPIRIT AND THE NATURAL

Exercise helps your heart; most of us were taught that at a young age in elementary school. Most of us learned many of the benefits of exercising as we got older. For example: exercising removes stress, lowers your blood pressure and keeps your cholesterol down. It will help you keep your body fit and weight down. Well, I have learned that there are numerous benefits from exercising in the spirit too. It directs your attention and your heart toward God which will keep you spiritually healthy and you will not be overcome by negative spiritual heavy weights. When your heart beats after the Lord, the grace of God will sustain you more. Now, you can reap more spiritual benefits that will affect your body. Now, the peace of God can overtake your mind. His joy and love can remove negative feelings of doubt, fear and depression.

Just like in the natural, your body sometimes does not feel like exercising. Why? Because exercising and eating healthy doesn't always feel good to your natural man. Most people are used to eating and living a lifestyle of however they want. However, we all need discipline in our lives; having some kind of discipline in your life can bring balance. So, if we get out of our comfort zone and see the whole picture and follow God's plan for our lives, we could ultimately save ourselves from a lot of heartache, setbacks and pain.

Usually, when a person first starts exercising, they complain about how hard the process is and how sore their body is. After a while though, once someone gets over the first couple of hurdles, their body doesn't seem to ache as much anymore. Then not only you, but others begin to see the results. *"But the LORD said to Samuel, 'Do not consider his appearance or his height, for I have rejected him. The LORD does not look at the things people look at. People look at the outward appearance, but the LORD looks at the heart'"* (I Samuel 16:7 NIV).

I believe God want us to look good on the outside, but He wants your heart and your character (your insides) to be a display for others to experience the true love and freedom of God too. Whatever is going on internally usually will manifest externally. We want God to do a transformation in us—inside and out. So many times, people get caught up in their looks which can lead to vanity and other negative things. I believe the Lord wants us to be a nice size, but we don't have to be a pencil stick and constantly compare ourselves to others. When people are always in competition, that's when they tend to get out of control and all kinds of negative behaviors and habits begin to creep into their hearts.

Portion sizes in your eating habits can naturally connect with trust issues spiritually. Sometimes, people over eat because they don't think they are going to get anymore. People also tend to over eat because they are trying to quench a thirst and hunger that can never be satisfied in our natural bodies. Jesus Christ, our Heavenly Father, is the only one who can fill that deep-down empty void in your life.

The opposite of eating too much, as you know, is not eating enough. There are people dealing with eating disorder issues as well. Whether you eat too much or if you don't eat enough, engaging in either of these behaviors will lead to you feeling weighted down. People who do not eat enough have a picture in their mind that they weigh too much, despite what they see in the mirror. That is an example of someone's mind heavily weighted down by toxic-poisonous negative thoughts about their image and outer appearance. The solution is you need God to help you transform your thinking about yourself. You need to see yourself the way God sees you. *"Thank you for making me so wonderfully complex! Your workmanship is marvelous—how well I know it"* (Psalm 139:14 NLT).

Whatever issues you are dealing with, Jesus can help you solve them. The root of the problem can be severed. Dealing with the real issue of the problem is the start of the process of the new you.

Everyone responds to various foods and exercises differently. Whether you know it or not, we all have a relationship with food. The foods we eat make us feel a certain way (happy, excited, comforted) and that is why we eat them. Exercise makes us feel a certain way when we first start (tired, sore, overwhelmed, intimidated) and that's why some of us don't like to do it. We would rather feel pleasure than discomfort.

Too many moments of pleasure can lead you to becoming sick to your stomach. We naturally want to feel good and we should. But, what cost do you have to pay for a moment to feel good? How many heavy bricks are you adding to your already overwhelming life? The Holy Spirit is a guide to help us make wise decisions that can keeps us free from engaging in behaviors that will weigh us down. Some people don't like the word "discipline," but if we ask God to help us and give us a passion for His will, we will soon learn that having some discipline in our lives will set us free.

THE RIGHT ATTITUDE AND HEART

I stated earlier that having the right heart and mind is essential to you overcoming and maintaining daily success. Too much competitiveness can be your destruction. Constantly comparing yourself to others will put you in a state of mind that is detrimental. *"Therefore, since we also have such a large cloud of witnesses surrounding us, let us lay aside every hindrance and the sin that so easily ensnares us. Let us run with endurance the race that lies before us, keeping our eyes on Jesus, the source and perfecter of our faith..."* (Hebrews 12:1-2 CSB).

You were made to be you and no one else! Don't ever forget who you belong to and who originally created you. Negative thoughts, at times, will creep into our minds to make us feel bad about ourselves and the way we look. These thoughts will make us forget that we are loved and made with a purpose and we were not made to be sad and depressed. The enemy of our soul specializes in using negative emotions to make us feel guilty about ourselves. He wants us to feel guilty about what we've done and how we don't measure up to others. Guilt sometimes has a relationship with anger, but God wants to deal with us about that so we can be free. So, because He loves us He also chastises us. (Hebrews 12:6-7 NIV).

There are things in all our hearts that mean us no good and hinder us from moving forward. We tend to cover up our inside flaws with a great looking outer appearance. When we see pictures and images of other people in magazines or on social media that make them look really good, we sometimes don't really understand that we have been tricked. If we are constantly trying to measure ourselves by false glamour pictures, then we will always be unhappy and deep down inside of us we will harbor feelings of incompleteness.

Throughout the years, I have noticed how commercials that promote weight loss tend to only show before and after pictures of their clients. It's great to look at people before and after, but we should also concentrate on the in between process. This is the chapter of the book we tend to leave out because usually we want a quick fix. One of the keys to keeping yourself on track is to know that God is with you during each phase of your weight loss process. There will be moments that you don't feel like working out or eating healthy, but your Heavenly Father is always there to help you become the best you.

Whether you know it or not, past situations that have broken our hearts hinder our weight loss process in the spirit and the natural. Some of us have tried so many times to recover from what has been done to us. But because we always tried to heal things our way, the pain always seems to resurface again and again. Today, make a choice to get rid of toxic thoughts about yourself and others; forgive yourself and others. The struggles in your life will NO longer hold you back, but you can use them today to be a breaking point into one of your many victories. *"but He has said to me, 'My grace is sufficient for you [My lovingkindness and My mercy are more than enough—always available—regardless of the situation]; for [My] power is being perfected [and is completed and shows itself most effectively] in [your] weakness.' Therefore, I will gladly boast in my weaknesses, so that the power of Christ [may completely enfold me and] may dwell in me"* (II Corinthians 12:9 AMP).

Your life is not a reality T.V. show to be broken up into multiple 30 minute episodes, so everyone can think you are perfect. Having some imperfections can lead to you being perfected as you learn and grow. Some changes concerning you will come quickly and other changes may take some time. But whatever transformation and renovation of you that takes place by the spirit of God, He can and will make them last a lifetime if you let Him.

A right heart and a made-up mind to be free will help you get through whatever you are dealing with every time. A right heart towards the Lord and the right attitude during the process of losing weight adds more grace to your weight loss process. Now, you are ready to lose weight physically and naturally. There is grace for you if you mess up. Remember, it's okay if you do. When you make a mistake with your weight loss process or in any area of your life, you have to use it as a learning opportunity; it's a time for you to grow and mature. People tend to revert back to their old habits because of how they feel. Our emotions and our feelings play a big role in our everyday life. But your feelings cannot rule you. Feelings will come and go, but the word of God will last and stand forever.

Your walk and relationship with God are not just about feelings all the time. Your relationship with the Lord is sometimes about going on what you know. What does the Bible say about you and your personal situations? God believes in you. The Lord does not make mistakes and you are an investment to Him. He spent time making you PERFECT with a purpose when He first made you. The word "perfect" means entirely without fault, fashioned by His reflection. Now, it's up to you to walk in His character daily.

You see, every day we live and move in a fleshly body that wants to do and live any way it wants. This soulish man loves to be separate from God and does not want to connect with Him. But when you get born again, your spirit man reconnects with God and what He intended from the beginning of time—can be manifested.

"For God so [greatly] loved and dearly prized the world, that He [even] gave His [One and] only begotten Son, so that whoever believes and trusts in Him [as Savior] shall not perish, but have eternal life" (John 3:16 AMP).

The Lord made the heavens and He also made you. He is truly worthy of all the glory. Keeping this kind of attitude and having a perfect heart towards the Lord will keep you blameless and take you a long way. With that being said, if you forget that God was the one who gave you grace and the mindset to start eating healthy and working out, in many ways you are setting yourself up for failure and opening yourself up to the spirit of pride and self exhortation. *"First pride, then the crash—the bigger the ego, the harder the fall"* (Proverbs 16:18 MSG).

HIS GRACE WILL HELP YOU OVERCOME

We all need grace daily; Lord knows I do! "Grace" is defined by the Merriam Webster as unmerited divine assistance given to humans for their regeneration or sanctification; a virtue coming from God.[1] Grace was given to us in the form of a gift that we do not deserve.

Human efforts will only you get you so far in life. You can do some things by your own will and power. You must understand that some battles have to be fought spiritually. If you let His spirit lead and guide you, His grace will always pull you through.

"... and then he told me, My grace is enough; it's all you need. My strength comes into its own in your weakness. Once I heard that, I was glad to let it happen. I quit focusing on the handicap and began appreciating the gift. It was a case of Christ's strength moving in on my weakness. Now I take limitations in stride, and with good cheer, these limitations that cut me down to size—abuse, accidents, opposition, bad breaks. I just let Christ take over! And so the weaker I get, the stronger I become" (II Corinthians 12:9 MSG).

His awesome sustaining power is better than your will power. He has enough grace for you when you fall or make a mistake. Problems and difficulties with your weight or any area you struggle with in your life is just an avenue used by God to help your dependence on Christ. It's just a strength training exercise to draw you closer to Him.

---

[1] "Grace." *Merriam-Webster* accessed November 20, 2019, https://www.merriam-webster.com.

I have written this book to help you become whole, new and complete. Transformed thinking comes about by meditating on the word of God and His truths for your life. When we focus on negative thoughts, we become weighted down spiritually which can result in natural weight gain. Today is your day to be free! Stop trying to put your stamp of approval on how things should be done. Too many times, we get in the way of ourselves; tripping over stuff that we should be free from, going around the same mountain, and tired of being sick and tired.

Many people want to be free and want to live a fulfilled life, but they just don't know how. Many people ask themselves and others questions like: How do I overcome this stumbling block? How come it seems like when I try to do everything right in my life, stuff seems to still fall apart? I was doing really good in that area and now I'm back in the same cycle again. How do I get over this hump, especially this weight loss mountain?

In order to get over the hump you are experiencing, you are going to have to learn how to walk in God's grace and love. See yourself and others the way God sees everything He made. In order for the weight loss process to work in your life, you need grace. Don't get me wrong, you do need discipline and self-control, and you probably need some kind of workout routine. But it's the grace of God that will sustain you and help you in the long run. His Divine "Grace" can be defined by Wikipedia-The Free Encyclopedia as His influence operating in humans to regenerate and sanctify, to inspire virtuous impulse, and to impart strength to endure trials and resist temptation.[2]

Natural exercise and spiritual exercise can be a way of life. God's personal fitness plan for you will leave you feeling light and free naturally and spiritually.

"But because God was so gracious, so very generous, here I am. And I'm not about to let his grace go to waste. Haven't I worked hard trying to do more than any of the others? Even then, my work didn't amount to all that much. It was God giving me the work to do, God giving me the energy to do it. So whether you heard it from me or from those others, it's all the same" (I Corinthians 15:10-11 MSG).

Losing weight naturally and spiritually go hand in hand. Anytime you make up in your mind that you are going to lose weight and change your outer appearance, you must first change your way of thinking. Your old mindset will not work with the new you. You can be brand new on the outside, but if your mind is still stuck in a rut on how you used to be and the way you used to think about yourself, you will always revert back to the old you that had you down in the dumps.

A spiritual, confident, encouraged mind through Christ Jesus will help you WIN every time! How do I know? I am your proof of the benefits of listening to my personal trainer. Don't just hear your personal trainer, listen to Him attentively! After all, you are a masterpiece, a work of art. *"For we are his workmanship, created in Christ Jesus for good works, which God prepared beforehand, that we should walk in them"* (Ephesians 2:10 ESV).

---

[2] "Grace in Christianity." *Wikipedia*, accessed November 22, 2019, https://en.wikipedia.org/wiki/Grace_in_Christianity.

Why wouldn't you take advice from the one who originally created you? He knows everything about you and I. He's not like man who sometimes doesn't want anything to do with us after we have messed up a couple of times. He constantly gives us a grace and wants us to start again, no matter how many times we may have made mistakes in the past. That's the great thing about being in relationship with Him. His friendship is like no other. *"I do not call you servants any longer, for the servant does not know what his master is doing; but I have called you [My] friends, because I have revealed to you everything that I have heard from My Father"* (John 15:15 AMP).

Your Heavenly Father wants the best for you, predestined you before the foundations of the world to complete a great work on this earth. God's love for you is your greatest defense against the negative demonic forces you face. He never ever intended for you to feel like you are worthless, beneath or less than; but the enemy of your soul wants you to feel that way. The scriptures tell us in John 10:10 (NKJV), *"The thief does not come except to steal, and to kill, and to destroy. I have come that they may have life, and that they may have it more abundantly."*

Before I started living my PHIT for LIFE principles with purpose, I felt good about losing natural weight, but at times I knew there was still something missing. Embracing losing weight God's way really helped me lay aside emotional weights too. *"And I am certain that God, who began the good work within you, will continue his work until it is finally finished on the day when Jesus Christ returns"* (Philippians 1:6 NLT). I noticed that by losing weight God's way, I wasn't so stressed out about how many pounds I would lose one week and what I would need to do if I gained that much weight back. I stopped counting my calorie intake so much and just focused on His plans and His ways. *"Be anxious for nothing, but in everything by prayer and supplication, with thanksgiving, let your requests be made known to God; and the peace of God, which surpasses all understanding, will guard your hearts and minds through Christ Jesus"* (Philippians 4:6-7 NKJV).

Don't get me wrong; I'm not saying that those things don't matter. Those thoughts just didn't consume me anymore. Sometimes we can be our own worst critic, but the Lord helped me get delivered from my own self. And when I really embraced who I had become, I also became free from outside critics too. It is an awesome, beautiful thing to know how much God really loves you no matter how you look; and, because of His love, He constantly gives us grace and mercy every day.

Now, at this very moment, make a decision that "by His grace, with the help of the Lord, I will become <u>PHIT for LIFE</u>!" Let the Lord make a habitation in your heart. The Lord habitually makes people and things that He loves. Whatever He loves, He purposed for it to do well. There is an even better version of you. You might not know it, but God knows it. Your best days are ahead of you, your future is bright, and you can do all things through Christ who strengthens you (Philippians 4:13 NKJV).

PHIT FOR LIFE HEALTH TIPS

Here are some healthy tips I use daily

- **Drink Plenty of Water**: Your body is made up of 70% water. I have researched, studied, and prayed about how others and I can become healed from many diseases. In my conclusion, I learned that drinking water can help cleanse the body of toxins, promotes cardiovascular health, hydrates the body, and helps cells function properly.

- **Grocery Shopping**: When you are grocery shopping, try to read the food labels of the items you purchase. Avoid foods that are high in sodium and sugar. Read the ingredient labels. Fresh produce products are always good healthy choices. Try not to go down the soda or cookie isle.

- **Start Healthy Habits with Your Kids and Your Family Today**: Making good habits will help you become consistent with making healthy choices. If you do not buy junk food and bring it home, you won't be tempted as much when you are home to eat junk food because it's not accessible. Pray and ask God to give you an open mind to try different fruits and vegetables. If you never step out of the box and engage in new behaviors, you will more than likely get the same results you always had.

- **Fruits and Vegetables are from the Earth**: The Bible tells us in Genesis 1:1 that the Lord made the heavens and the earth. Since the beginning of time, the earth has produced many plants that have healed people naturally. I personally believe if we pray and ask God about the foods we should and should not eat, we can live a whole, fulfilled, healthy life.

- **Stay Mentally Sound with the Word of God**: Whatever you focus on, meditate on and spend time with will become a part of you. If you practice negative thoughts, you will become negative. If you practice saying what God says about you and walking in love, joy and peace, positive behaviors will be a part of your behavior and everyday lifestyle.

PHIT FOR LIFE HEALTHY MEALS

Who says you can't eat healthy meals that taste good

Ever since I was a little girl, I always enjoyed watching cooking channels. Some of the cooking shows I watched were healthy and some were not. Even though I loved watching people cook, I wasn't always pressed about getting in the kitchen.

A couple years after my husband and I got married, I went to the doctor for a check-up and she later shared with me some disturbing health news about my body. The doctor wanted to put me on various medicines (like a trial and error period). I just came out and told her I'm not going to do that. I am going to go home and pray for healing in my body, a desire to exercise and healthy ways to change my diet. Over the next couple of weeks, I did so. The awesome thing was my hubby began to make healthy lifestyle changes too.

When I went back to the doctor, she was amazed that I actually did what I said I was going to do. Not only had I lost weight, but I was healed from the disease that attacked my body.

Here are some healthy, tasty recipes I have used for over 13 years. They are quick and easy to prepare. I created some of them; others are from family, friends, and the internet.

PHIT for LIFE Shrimp Egg Rolls Recipe

Serves: 3 to 4   Prep Time: 25 mins
                 Cook Time: 25 mins

Instructions

1. Heat tablespoon of olive oil in a skillet. Add your cabbage, broth and carrots to the pan (cook 3 to 4 minutes)
2. Next put your shrimp into the pan, soy sauce, oyster sauce, cayenne pepper, black pepper and garlic powder (cook 4 to 5 minutes)
3. Add your mixture to the middle of the egg roll wrap. Fold bottom corner over filling; roll tightly hallway and cover filling. Fold in both sides of the wrap into the middle. Moisten edges with some water; use your fingertips to do this. Finish rolling the wrap and seal
4. Preheat your oven to 400 degrees
5. Repeat this process for the rest of your egg rolls. Place on backing sheet or in a pan. Baked the egg rolls for 25 minutes and enjoy!

Notes

- Cabbages are rich in antioxidants and help with skin blemishes.

Ingredients

- 1 package of egg roll wraps
- 2 cups of cabbage shredded
- 1/2 lb. of shrimp
- 1 carrot shredded
- 1 1/2 tablespoon of soy sauce or Asian sauce
- 1 teaspoon of oyster sauce (optional)
- 1 tablespoon of olive oil
- 1/4 ounce of chicken or bone broth
- 1/2 teaspoon of cayenne pepper, black pepper and garlic powder

PHIT for LIFE Shrimp and Spinach Salad Recipe

Serves: 1 to 2   Prep Time: 10 mins
                 Cook Time: 15 mins

Instructions

1. Wash and dry spinach or salad. Remove stems from spinach and place into a large bowl
2. Boil the eggs for 10 to 15 minutes
3. Pat your shrimp dry and season with garlic and pepper. Grill or cook in a medium heated pan with a little olive oil (optional) until pink on both sides (4 to 5 minutes)
4. Add your cooked shrimp to your spinach or regular salad
5. Slice your tomatoes in half and add them to your salad along with your almonds or pecans
6. Remove your boiled eggs from water. Dry and cut in half. Spoon out the boiled egg (egg shell peeling should come right off)
7. Top with a small amount of dressing and enjoy!

Notes

- Eating salads are good choice to a healthy diet.
- Salads are low in sodium and do not contain a lot of cholesterol.

Ingredients

- 8 ounces salad or spinach
- 2 boiled eggs
- 4 to 5 ounces of shrimps
- 5 cherry tomatoes
- Handful of almonds or pecans
- 1/4 teaspoon of garlic and pepper
- Small amount of dressing of your choice

PHIT for LIFE Turkey Bacon Vegetable Quiche Recipe

Serves: 3 to 4   Prep Time: 25 mins
                  Cook Time: 25 mins

Ingredients

- 4 eggs
- Half an onion
- 2/3 cup of mushroom
- 1/4 cup of zucchini (optional)
- 1 cup of crème or milk
- 1 deep dish pie crust
- 5 slices of turkey bacon
- 1 cup of chopped spinach
- 1 cup of mixed shredded cheese
- 1/2 teaspoon of salt and pepper
- 1 tablespoon of olive oil

Instructions

1. Cook your turkey bacon in a pan until done. Chop up your bacon and put to the side for later (chop spinach up as well)
2. Heat olive oil in a pan over medium heat. Cook and stir chopped onion, mushrooms and zucchini (7 minutes or until soft)
3. Preheat oven to 375 degrees
4. In a small bowl, whisk together eggs, crème, salt, and pepper
5. In the bottom of the pie crust, shell spread chopped spinach and turkey bacon. Then put in cooked onions, mushrooms and zucchini. Add your eggs and crème. Sprinkle shredded cheese on top
6. Cook your quiche for 25 minutes and enjoy!

Notes

- This is an easy way to make breakfast in a different way.

PHIT for LIFE Homemade Breakfast Pizza

Serves: 3 to 4   Prep Time: 20 mins
                           Cook Time: 12 mins

Instructions

1. Lay flat one whole wheat tortilla on a baking sheet or a piece of aluminum foil for backing
2. Cook your turkey bacon or sausage in a pan until done
3. Add a little olive oil to your pan and cook your onions and mushrooms on medium high for 7 to 10 minutes
4. Crack your eggs into a bowl and mix in your milk. Scramble your eggs but leave them a little runny
5. On your flat tortilla, sprinkle some of your shredded cheese, add your eggs all around the pizza (leave a little room for the crust). Finally, add your turkey bacon or turkey sausage, chopped onions, mushrooms, and spinach if you like.
6. Bake at 400 degrees for 12 minutes and enjoy!

Notes

- Flat bread or thin crust pizzas have less calories than regular dough pizzas.

Ingredients

- 1 whole wheat tortilla
- 3 slices of turkey bacon or 3 ounces of turkey sausage
- 1/4 of a chopped onion
- 1/4 cup of mushrooms
- 3 eggs
- 1/4 cup of milk
- Handful of spinach
- 1/3 cup of shredded cheese
- 1 tablespoon of olive oil

PHIT for LIFE Homemade Vegetable Meat Pizza

Serves: 3 to 4   Prep Time: 20 mins
                 Cook Time: 15 mins

Instructions

1. Lay flat one whole wheat tortilla on a baking sheet or a piece of aluminum foil for backing
2. Cook your turkey bacon or other meat in a pan until almost done
3. Add a little olive oil to your pan and cook your bell pepper, onions and mushrooms on medium high for 7 to 10 minutes
4. On your flat tortilla, add your sauce in a circular motion, sprinkle your shredded cheese, add all of your other toppings (leave a little room for the crust). Finally, add your oregano on top
5. Bake at 400 degrees for 12 minutes and enjoy!

Notes

- Family members are more likely to eat healthy meals together when healthy meals are prepared together while just having fun.

Ingredients

- 1 whole wheat tortilla or regular tortilla
- 2 slices of turkey bacon or any meat you like
- 1/2 teaspon oregano
- Goat cheese or regular mozzarella cheese
- Handful of spinach
- 1/4 of a bell pepper
- 1/4 of an onion
- 1/4 cup of mushrooms
- 1/4 cup of marinara or tomato sauce

PHIT for LIFE Pineapple and Kale Juice

Serves: 1 to 2   Prep Time: 10 mins
             Total Time: 10 mins

Instructions

1. Peel, core and cut into big pieces the ripe fresh pineapple. Add pieces to the juicer
2. Wash the kale and chop them roughly. Add them to the juicer too
3. Juice them together

Notes

- Fresh kale provides vitamin A, vitamin K, vitamin C, vitamin B6, calcium, potassium, and magnesium.
- Pineapple juice benefits are anti-inflammatory properties, vitamin C, gut and heart health.

Ingredients

- 1/4 fresh pineapple and cut it into chunks
- 4 kale leaves, fresh, roughly chopped

PHIT for LIFE Strawberry Ginger Lemonade Juice

Serves: 1   Prep Time: 10 mins
                 Total Time: 10 mins

Instructions

1. Peel ginger and cut 1 to 2 slices. Add pieces to the juicer
2. Add strawberries to juicer
3. Add lemons to juicer
4. Juice them together

Notes

- Studies have shown ginger can reduce pain, aids in digestion and helps with inflammation.

Ingredients

- 10 to 12 strawberries
- 2 slices of lemon
- 2 slices of ginger

PHIT for LIFE Apple Cucumber with Celery Juice

Serves: 1 to 2   Prep Time: 10 mins
                  Total Time: 10 mins

Instructions

1. Cut apples in half and add to juicer
2. Add your cucumber
3. Add your celery stick
4. Juice them together

Notes

- Celery contains high levels of vitamin K and vitamin A.
- Apples are low in sodium and a good source of vitamin C.

Ingredients

- 1 1/2 apple
- 1 cucumber
- 1 celery stick

PHIT for LIFE Banana Smoothie

Serves: 1 to 2   Prep Time: 10 mins
                  Total Time: 10 mins

Instructions

1. In a high speed blender, combine all of the smoothie ingredients
2. Blend until smooth and creamy. Enjoy immediately!

Notes

- Bananas are rich in potassium and can help manage your blood pressure.

Ingredients

- 1 1/2 banana
- 1 cup of milk or almond milk
- 1 teaspoon of vanilla extract
- 1/4 cup of ice

PHIT for LIFE Blueberry Spinach Smoothie

Serves: 1 to 2   Prep Time: 10 mins
                 Total Time: 10 mins

Instructions

1. Add all ingredients into the blender
2. Blend until smooth and creamy. Enjoy immediately!

Notes

- Blueberries contain iron, phosphorous, calcium, magnesium, and zinc.
- Spinach is an excellent source of vitamin A, vitamin K, vitamin B2, and folate.

Ingredients

- 1 cup of spinach leaves
- 1 cup of milk of choice
- 1 teaspoon of honey
- 2/3 cup of blueberries
- 2/3 cup of Greek yogurt
- 1/4 cup of ice

PHIT for LIFE Kiwi Strawberry Smoothie

Serves: 1 to 2   Prep Time: 10 mins
　　　　　　　　Total Time: 10 mins

Instructions

1. Add all ingredients into the blender
2. Blend until smooth and creamy. Enjoy immediately!

Notes

- Kiwi has fiber and vitamin C.
- Strawberries contain many antioxidants and fiber.

Ingredients

- 1 kiwi
- 5 strawberries
- 1/2 cup of vanilla yogurt
- 1/4 cup of ice

EXERCISE TIPS

1. **Have Fun!!**: Pray for an anointing and grace to enjoy working out. If you always think of working out as a hard task and something you don't want to do it, you probably will not do it.

2. **Listen to Music**: Listening to music will help you stay motivated; especially when your workouts become difficult. I really like listening to Christian Hip Hop, Contemporary Christian music, and Gospel music. You need music that will inspire you and push you to be better.

3. **Get a Workout Partner or an Exercise App**: A good workout partner will motivate and encourage you to keep exercising. Today, society has so many ways for you to connect with other people even if you are not face to face with someone. Many exercise apps will give you a variety of different workouts so you will not get bored and they can send you friendly reminders about exercising.

4. **Exercise at a Pace Good for You**: Stay focused on your plan and what is best for you. There will be times when you may work out or exercise really hard; then there will be times when you may not workout hard. The key is to not compare yourself to other people. Your strength should come from God, not from trying to be like someone else.

PHIT FOR LIFE EXERCISE PLANS

WEEK ONE

Day 1

- ➢ 10 high knees, 10 jumping jacks, 10 lunges, 15 sit ups, 10 second plank (rest break)
- ➢ Repeat
- ➢ Repeat and stretch

Day 2

- ➢ If you are able, take 10 to 20-minute jog or walk in your neighborhood or on the treadmill/elliptical

Day 3

- ➢ 15 front kicks, 10 push-ups, 7 burpees, 20 sit ups, 10 mountain climbers (rest break)
- ➢ Repeat
- ➢ Repeat and stretch

WEEK TWO

Day 1

- ➢ 15 lunges, 10 squats, 5 walking planks, 20 sit ups, 7 push-ups (rest break)
- ➢ Repeat
- ➢ Repeat and stretch

Day 2

- ➢ Jump rope intervals (Jump rope for 30 seconds and then rest; repeat 2 more times)

- 15 min walk or jog on the treadmill or outside

Day 3

- Solider man walk (8), 10 arm circles forward and back (try not to bring your arms down), 8 shoulder planks, 20 jumping jacks (rest break)
- Repeat
- Repeat and stretch

WEEK THREE

Day 1

- 15 high knees, 25 sit ups, 8 burpees, 15 lunges, 15 mountain climbers (rest break)
- Repeat
- Repeat and stretch

Day 2

- If you have cones or any object, lay them in your driveway or an open space in your house about 10 feet apart
- Run forward to one cone and then run backward (5 times)
- Side shuffle back and forth and touch the cone when you get to each end (5 times)
- Take a 15-minute walk or jog

Day 3

- 10 leg raise each leg while laying on your side, 10 front kicks, combination punches (left jab, right punch, 10 times), 20 uppercut punches, (rest break)
- Repeat

- ➢ Repeat and stretch

WEEK FOUR

Day 1

- ➢ 25 jumping jacks, 30 sit ups, 30 lunges, 10 burpees, 15 arm circles front and back (rest break)
- ➢ Repeat
- ➢ Repeat and stretch

Day 2

- ➢ Walk for 10 minutes, jog for 10 minutes, run for 10 minutes (at the park, neighborhood, treadmill, your preference)

Day 3

- ➢ 10 walking planks, 25 squats, 20 push ups, 20 elbow knee touches, speed skate exercise (move your arms and your legs as if you are speed skating while staying in the same spot 20 times)
- ➢ Repeat
- ➢ Repeat and stretch

ABOUT THE AUTHOR

Tiffany James is the founder of PHIT for LIFE with Purpose, a Physical Education teacher, former youth director at her church for 14 years, motivational speaker, Minister of the Gospel, musician, and a servant for the Kingdom of God. She lives with her husband, two children and her dog.

Years before writing this book, she was unhappy with her current job. She went back to school and received a Bachelor's Degree in Health Promotion and Wellness from the University of North Carolina Wilmington. It helped her become a Physical Education teacher.

Teaching has allowed her to be a coach, encourage students mentally and physically, implement fitness clubs, host walk and run events, organize motivational seminars with Chuck Mammay (an American Ninja Warrior), and host workshops with great influential leaders.

Throughout the years, organizing events has ignited a passion in her to help people become healthy and free God's way. Her goal is to motivate everyone she comes in contact with to be the best version of what God has called them to be through Christ Jesus.

You can connect with Tiffany, watch health tip videos, and check out PHIT4LIFE apparel on her website at phit4lifewpurpose.com.

www.ingramcontent.com/pod-product-compliance
Lightning Source LLC
Chambersburg PA
CBHW071916070526
44583CB00016B/2022